Mali Under the Night Sky

A Lao Story of Home

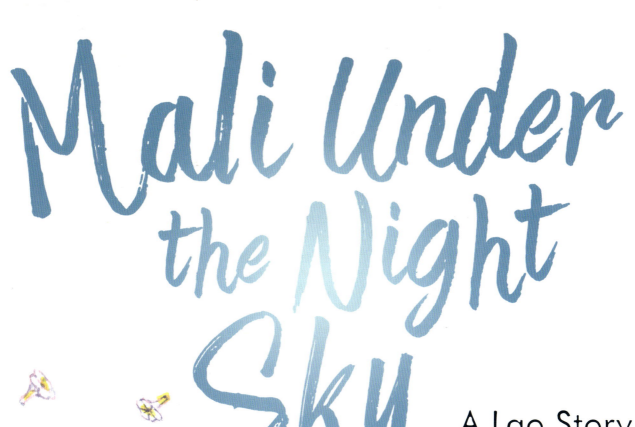

Written and illustrated by
YOUME

Cinco Puntos Press
An imprint of LEE & LOW BOOKS INC.
New York

When Mali was very young, she already knew that the world was big—*yai*—and full of wonderful things.

She loved to sit in front of her house and ask everyone,
"Where are you going—*jao si pai sai?*"

Catching tiny fish in the rice field.
Quick, quick—*vai, vai!*

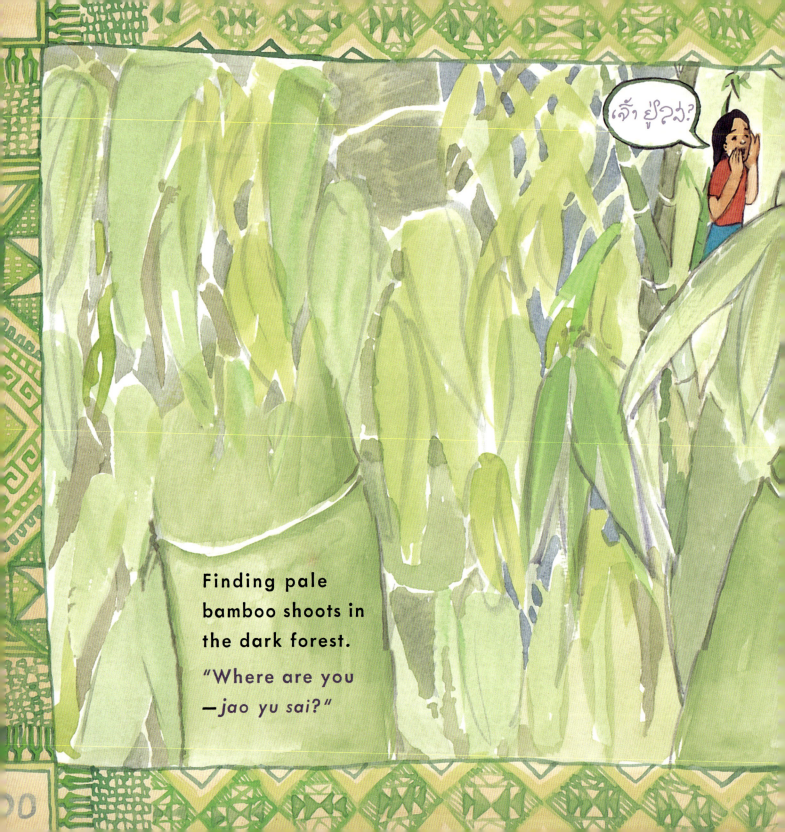

Finding pale bamboo shoots in the dark forest.

"Where are you —*jao yu sai?*"

Napping with her family during the hottest time of the day.
Shhhhhhh…

She loved to make feasts with her aunts, spicy hot and delicious—*saep lai!*

On very special days, for weddings, or when someone was traveling far away, family and friends gathered to eat, to dance together, and to tie strings around one another's wrists.

This was a way of showing that their hearts would always be together.

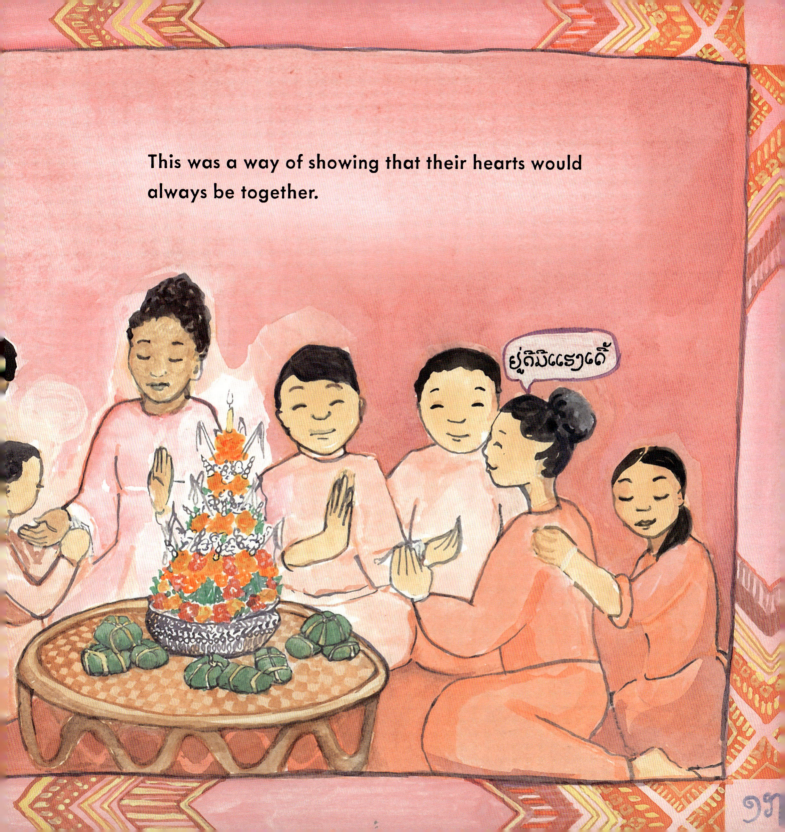

But something was changing where Mali lived. People stopped going everywhere.

No one sat outside their houses to greet their friends. Fighting in neighboring countries was bringing danger to the land and the people. Even the birds were disappearing.

One night, the strings were for Mali and her family. Mali wondered—would she be leaving her home?

That night, Mali listened to her parents, grandparents, aunts, and uncles talking. "You have to take the children. No one is safe here. The war is getting closer."

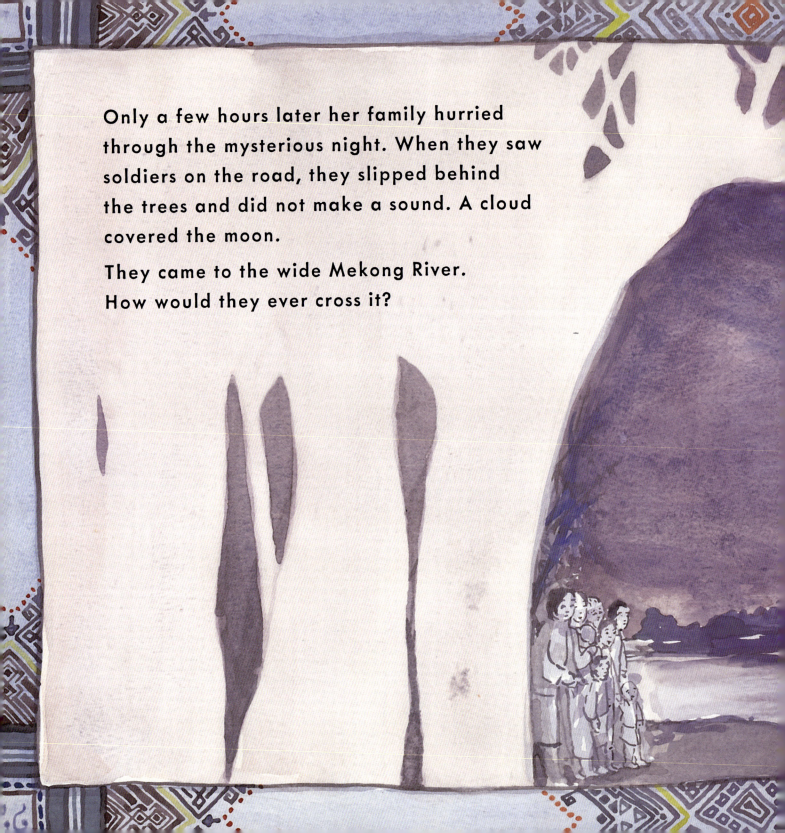

Only a few hours later her family hurried through the mysterious night. When they saw soldiers on the road, they slipped behind the trees and did not make a sound. A cloud covered the moon.

They came to the wide Mekong River. How would they ever cross it?

Mali felt her father's strong arms lift her up and put her into a small wooden boat. The clouds passed and the clear round moon shone high in the sky, reflecting on the water and the family quietly crossing.

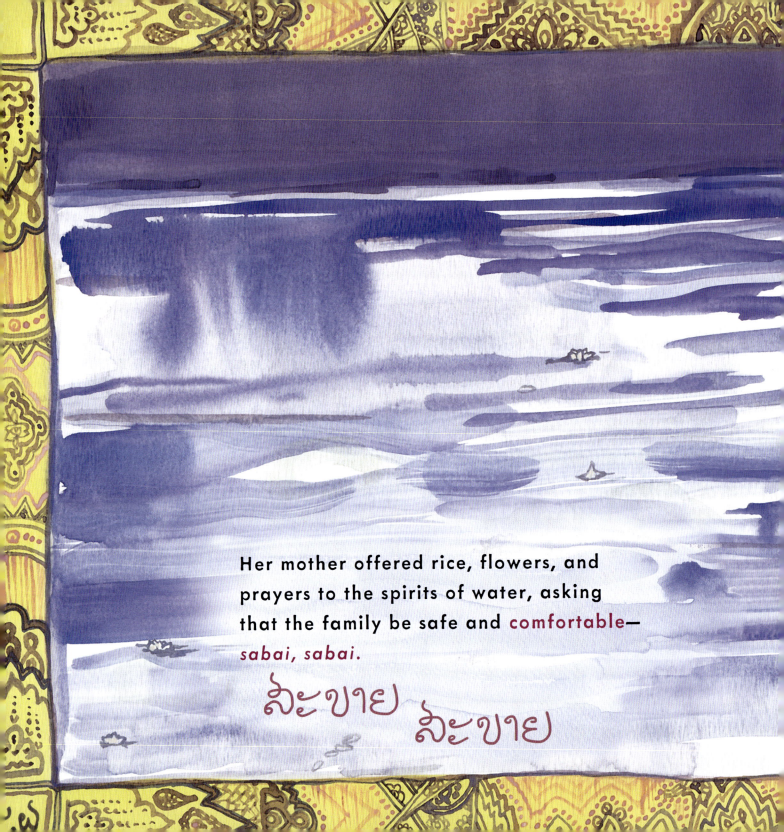

Her mother offered rice, flowers, and prayers to the spirits of water, asking that the family be safe and **comfortable**— *sabai, sabai.*

ສະບາຍ ສະບາຍ

They slept outside that night in a banana grove, where the broad, soft leaves let the blue moonlight through. Mali and her family were so tired, yet they were glad to feel safe together beneath the full moon.

But the other side of the river was a new country. And when they woke up, they found themselves lost with so many other traveling families. Men came and arrested them for not having a home.

Now Mali was in the worst place she had ever been, a crowded jail. Angry, tired jailers. No flowers, no fish. No trees and no home.

Was everything lost to her?

Mali looked at her wrists and saw the strings that tied her to her beautiful home. She told everyone in the jail her memories. Everyone who heard her felt that they too were climbing trees, catching fish, and feeling both free and loved. They remembered their own beautiful homes. And though the journey to a new home would be long and hard, their hearts were safe when they remembered where they had come from.

well being—*yu dee mee haeng der*

(Top) *Home*, 2003, 32″ x 48″, mixed media. (Bottom) *Self Portrait*, 2003, 32″ x 48″, mixed media. From the collection of the Family Housing Fund.

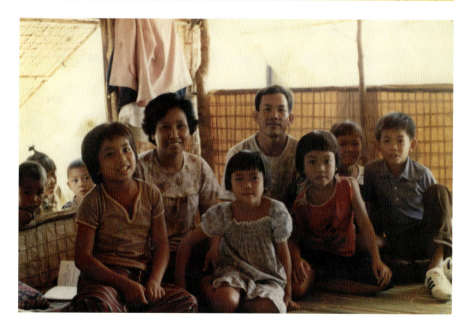

(Top) Mali, standing center, with her family in Wayzata, Minnesota, in 2021.
(Bottom) Mali, sitting center-right, with her family at Ubon Refugee Camp, Thailand, 1979.

"Healing the Wounds of War" by Thavisouk Phrasavath
As told to Jessica Powers

Laos is a country surrounded by other countries, sharing its borders with Myanmar (Burma) and China to the northwest, Vietnam to the east, Cambodia to the south, and Thailand to the west. I was born in 1964 in Laos during the civil war. There has never been a time without war for me.

I first realized I was in the middle of the war in a single moment. It was afternoon. The city was quiet. There was a bomb explosion. I looked up at the sky and I saw a rocket coming. All of a sudden, I saw someone blown away. Like dust, like one breath of life, she just disappeared in a second. I will never forget that moment.

A country much bigger than Laos was conducting a secret war in our country to build a defense against our neighboring country of Vietnam. That big country was America. For nine years, bombs were dropped on my country, one bombing mission every eight minutes.

When I was thirteen and a half, the Communists took over and many of us were forced to leave because of the political turmoil. My family and friends told me I had to leave Laos. I didn't know what was going to happen and I decided to escape. Circumstances brought me to America. There I was reunited with some, but not all, of my family.

Mali and I were both the children of war. What we experienced became the energy that drew us together as friends. We are not only bound by the atrocities of our war experience, but also because living in exile inspired us to be the kind of artists we are today. We transform our life experience, our cultural heritage, to create awareness and a tool for better understanding our histories.

Stories like *Mali Under the Night Sky* are a balm that will heal the wounds of the war. Our stories can vitally inspire victims of war to face their own history and to be able to let past tragedy and trauma be resolved. I am very sure Mali's story will find its own way to inspire the hearts and souls of victims of war, of refugees, of immigrants and asylum seekers all around the world.

Thavisouk Phrasavath is a writer, artist, and filmmaker. In 2008, he was nominated for both an Academy Award and a Film Independent Spirit Award.

Book and cover design by
Sergio A. Gómez and Elliane Mellet

Copyright © 2010 by Youme Landowne. Illustrations copyright © 2010 by Youme Landowne. All rights reserved. No part of this book may be reproduced, transmitted, or stored in an information retrieval system in any form or by any means, electronic, mechanical, photocopying, recording, or otherwise, without written permission from the publisher. Cinco Puntos Press, an imprint of LEE & LOW BOOKS Inc., 95 Madison Avenue, New York NY 10016, leeandlow.com

Production by The Kids at Our House
The text is set in Metallophile Sp8 Medium
Manufactured in Korea by Mirae-N

First Edition
PB 10 9 8 7 6 5 4 3 2 1   HC 10 9 8 7 6 5 4 3 2 1

Library of Congress Cataloging-in-Publication Data. Youme. Mali under the night sky : a Lao story of home / by Youme Landowne ; illustrated by Youme Landowne. — 1st ed. p. cm. Hardcover ISBN 978-1-93369-368-2 Paperback ISBN 978-1-64379-659-8 eBook ISBN 978-1-93595-519-1. 1. Kouanchao, Malichansouk, 1971—Juvenile literature. 2. Laotian American artists—Biography—Juvenile literature. I. Kouanchao, Malichansouk, 1971– II. Title. III. Title: Lao story of home. N6537.K655Y68 2010 709.2–dc22 [B] 2009042862

Thank you—*khop jai*
Soukanh, Chomsy, Chanda, Malaysi, Ketmani, and Soukthavi Kouanchao.
XiuDaen Maly Kongsisy, Mme Xuyên Dangers, Vin, Xay, TiFre, Hai, Song, and Tao!